LET'S WORK IT OUT™

How to deal with INSULTS

Julie Fiedler

PowerKiDS press™

New York

Published in 2007 by The Rosen Publishing Group, Inc.
29 East 21st Street, New York, NY 10010

Copyright © 2007 by The Rosen Publishing Group, Inc.

All rights reserved. No part of this book may be reproduced in any form without permission in writing from the publisher, except by a reviewer.

First Edition

Editor: Jennifer Way
Book Design: Ginny Chu
Book Layout: Kate Laczynski
Photo Researcher: Sam Cha

Photo Credits: All Photos Shutterstock.com.

Library of Congress Cataloging-in-Publication Data

Fiedler, Julie.
  How to deal with insults / Julie Fiedler.— 1st ed.
      p. cm. — (Let's work it out)
  Includes index.
  ISBN-13: 978-1-4042-3673-8 (lib. bdg.)
  ISBN-10: 1-4042-3673-2 (lib. bdg.)
  1. Interpersonal relations—Juvenile literature. 2. Invective—Juvenile literature. 3. Interpersonal relations in children—Juvenile literature. I. Title.
  HM1106.F54 2007
  158.2—dc22
                                        2006028556

Manufactured in the United States of America

Contents

Pine Road Library
Lower Moreland Township
Huntingdon Valley, Pa.

Insults can make people feel hurt, angry, or even sad.

What Is an Insult?

An insult is a mean thing someone says to hurt another person's feelings. People may use insults because they are angry, **jealous**, or have low **self-esteem**. Some people pick people who are different from others to insult. Others use insults instead of talking about their hurt feelings.

It is not good to insult people since it makes them feel bad. By learning why people use insults, you can learn to **avoid** insulting and hurting people.

The emotional pain of insults can last a long time.

Insults Hurt

Have you ever heard the saying "Sticks and stones can break my bones, but words can never hurt me"? Words cannot hurt you **physically**, but they can hurt you **emotionally**. Can you think of a time someone insulted you? It likely made you feel bad about yourself.

Insults do not help people show their emotions or **solve** their problems. You can deal with **situations** better by avoiding using insults and doing things that build self-esteem.

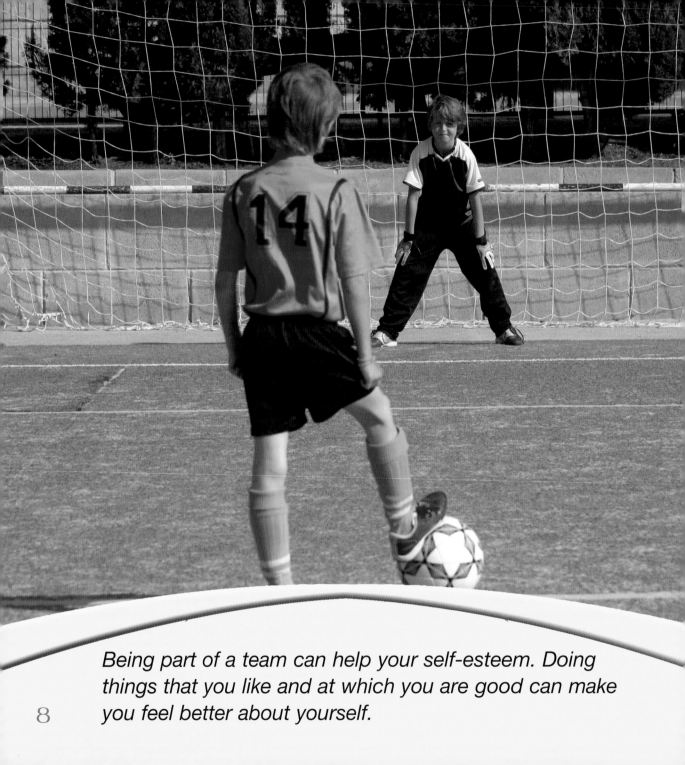

Being part of a team can help your self-esteem. Doing things that you like and at which you are good can make you feel better about yourself.

Self-Esteem

Self-esteem is your sense of your own value. Some people think putting others down and hurting their self-esteem will make them feel better. That is not true. Building a strong self-esteem will make you feel better about yourself.

You can build your self-esteem in many ways. Try listing things you are good at. Give yourself **compliments**. Love the things that make you special. When you have high self-esteem, you will not feel the need to use insults. If someone insults you, it will not hurt you as much.

Sometimes insecure people will take part in insulting another person when there is a group doing it.

Did Someone Insult You?

When someone insults you, you may want to insult the person back. That will not help because you will both feel worse. Things also could get out of control. It even could lead to a fight.

You should instead ask yourself why the other person is insulting you. Do you think he or she feels **insecure**, is angry at you, or is just being mean? Try to talk with that person. If you do not feel **comfortable** or safe, walk away. You can also talk to a trusted adult about your feelings.

If you are insulting others, it is important to understand why you are doing it. Then you can learn to deal with your feelings in a healthy way.

Do You Insult Others?

Have you ever insulted someone? It is important to understand why you did it so that you can avoid doing it again. Were you hurt, angry about something, or trying to get back at that person for something? How did you feel when you insulted them? Did you feel better, or did you feel bad that you had hurt someone's feelings? Did insulting someone solve a problem or just make someone feel bad?

You can learn to stop insulting others and deal with your problems in a healthy way. This will help make everyone feel better.

An apology is a good first step in talking out problems with others.

Apologizing

It is important to **apologize** if you hurt people's feelings. When you apologize, tell them you are sorry that you hurt their feelings. Tell them that you will do your best not to do it again. It is important to mean what you say when you apologize.

If they **accept** your apology, they will forgive you and everyone will feel better. If someone apologizes to you, you can accept the apology. If someone apologizes to you and then insults you again, you can try to talk it out with him.

Talking to an adult whom you trust can help you deal with your problems.

Talking It Out

If people insult you, they may be angry. Their insult may make you angry, too. It can be easy to get caught up in your anger. You might want to say something hurtful back. That will just make the problem worse. It is a good idea to wait until you are **calm** before talking to that person.

When you talk to the person who insulted you, tell her how the insult made you feel. If that does not work, talk to a friend or a trusted adult. He may help you work through your hurt feelings.

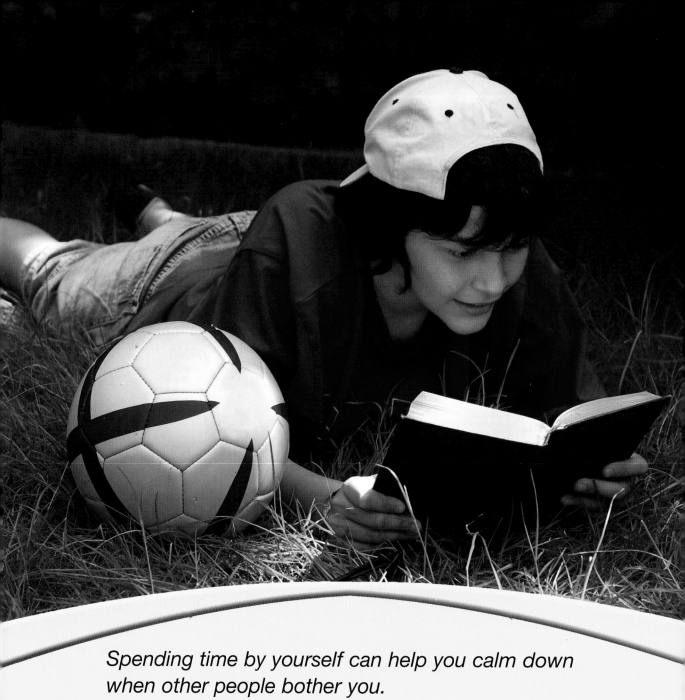

Spending time by yourself can help you calm down when other people bother you.

Taking a Break

If you are around others a lot, you may need to take a break just to have your own space. People who do not take a break may feel **stressed** and say mean things. Sometimes brothers, sisters, or close friends may start to bother you for no reason at all.

By giving yourself time out, you can avoid the stress that may cause you to use nasty insults that you do not mean. Everyone needs time alone sometimes. It is OK to ask to have time to yourself.

Sometimes the best thing to do when someone insults you is to walk away.

Walking Away

If someone insults you, do not fight or insult her back. You can just walk away. People who use insults to pick fights are called bullies.

If someone is insulting you often or if you are being bullied, tell an adult whom you trust. Tell him what happened, who hurt you, and how it made you feel. Adults can help the situation. Talking about the situation can help you start to feel better.

No More Insults

Everyone is different and special in their own way. When you have good self-esteem, you will like the things that make you special and feel good about yourself.

When you respect others, you can talk to them in a healthy way. Insults are mean and **disrespectful**. They only make people feel worse and do not solve problems. When you learn to talk about your feelings and problems in a healthy way, you show the world that you have respect for yourself and for other people.

Glossary

accept (ik-SEPT) To take what is offered.

apologize (uh-PAH-leh-jyz) To tell someone you are sorry.

avoid (uh-VOYD) To stay away from something.

calm (KAHLM) Peaceful.

comfortable (KUMF-ter-bul) Feeling OK about something.

compliments (KOM-pluh-ments) Something good that is said about one.

disrespectful (dis-rih-SPEKT-ful) Without consideration for someone.

emotionally (ih-MOH-shnuh-lee) Having to do with feelings.

insecure (in-seh-KYUR) Shy or uncertain.

jealous (JEH-lus) Wanting what someone else has.

physically (FIH-zih-kuh-lee) Having to do with the body.

self-esteem (self-uh-STEEM) Happiness with oneself.

situations (sih-choo-AY-shunz) Problems or things that happen.

solve (SOLV) To figure something out.

stressed (STREST) Worried or feeling bad because of a problem.

Index

Web Sites

Due to the changing nature of Internet links, PowerKids Press has developed an online list of Web sites related to the subject of this book. This site is updated regularly. Please use this link to access the list:

www.powerkidslinks.com/lwio/insult/